Supporting Children with Attention Deficit Hyperactivity Disorder

2nd Edition

Kate E. Spohrer

continuum

Continuum International Publishing Group

The Tower Building	80 Maiden Lane
11 York Road	Suite 704
London	New York
SE1 7NX	NY 10038

www.continuumbooks.com

First published by Questions Publishing Company 2003
Reprinted by Continuum 2005
Second edition published by Continuum 2006

Design by: Ivan Morrison
         James Davies
         John Minett
Cover photograph by: Amanda Greenley

With thanks to Sheila Thornton and the pupils at Hallmoor School in Birmingham for their kind permission to use the cover photograph.

British Library Cataloguing-in-Publication Data
A catalogue record for this book is available from the British Library.

ISBN: 0–8264–8077–2 (paperback)

Library of Congress Cataloging-in-Publication Data
Spohrer, Kate E.
   Supporting children with attention deficit hyperactivity disorder / Kate E. Spohrer.– 2nd ed.
      p. cm.
   Includes bibliographical references.
   ISBN 0–8264–8077–2 (pbk.)
  1. Attention-deficit hyperactivity disorder. 2. Attention-deficit hyperactivity disorder–Patients–Education. 3. Attention-deficit hyperactivity disorder--Patients–Rehabilitation. I. Title
   RJ506.H9S663 2006
   618.92'8589–dc22

                                        2005037805

Typeset by BookEns Ltd, Royston, Hertfordshire
Printed and bound in Great Britain by The Bath Press, Bath

Contents

Introduction

This is a book for all school staff, parents and carers of young people with attention deficit hyperactivity disorder (ADHD) or who exhibit ADHD type behaviour. Its primary aim is to provide a method for adults to work with these young people and to increase the young person's understanding of themselves.

Chapters 4 to 7 of this book contain activities and exercises for a pupil who has been diagnosed with ADHD, or whom you feel exhibits many of the characteristics of ADHD. They are ideally suited to a busy special educational needs coordinator (SENCo) who wants appropriate materials for their learning support staff who are working one-to-one with a pupil, and the activities will support targets in an individual education plan (IEP). In theory many of these exercises can be completed by the pupil independently. The major objective of the work is an increased understanding by the pupil of their own condition, and a subsequent improvement in executive function. Teachers and support staff who work through this book with a pupil will increase their understanding of the types of activity a pupil needs to practise. The activities are not exhaustive or definitive, but are examples that can act as a springboard for your own ideas. Included are exercises taken from many disciplines, for example yoga and art therapy.

In addition, in this second edition I have added a theoretical section on the background to ADHD, with a historical development of the term (Chapter 2). Included in this chapter are sections on medical and alternative therapies for the treatment of ADHD. What the Teacher Can Do (now Chapter 3) has also been expanded and includes an extensive section on writing an individual education plan for inclusion of a child with ADHD in the mainstream classroom.

Part 1: Information for School Staff, Parents and Carers

1 | What is ADHD?

Try to imagine being in a room where there is a radio in every corner, each one on a different channel, plus a team of construction workers outside digging the road, a flight path overhead, and windows giving full view of these passing aircraft and construction workers. Add the normal distractions found in any classroom, and you may begin to get a flavour of what it is like at times in the head of a person with an ADHD type personality. Knowing how to prioritize what to attend to first can be a great challenge, and very confusing.

Attention deficit hyperactivity disorder (ADHD) is a medical diagnosis given to children who have developmental, behavioural and cognitive difficulties compared to their peers. It is diagnosed using criteria from either the *International Classification of Diseases* 10, or *Diagnostic Statistical Manual* IV.

ADHD has three components:

- sustaining attention and concentration
- controlling impulses
- controlling motor activity.

A diagnosis is only correctly made when there are problems in these areas over and above those found in the peer group and in more than one setting.

ADHD type behaviour is found in most people at some time, the factors changing such behaviour into ADHD being persistence, pervasiveness and intensity. It is thought that the root of the problem lies in the inability to inhibit behaviour. So, for example, we might have a fleeting thought: 'I wonder what it would be like to jump out of this 14-storey window?' Before you know it an ADHD child could have tried this out!

A child born with an ADHD disposition will attract much negative feedback for their actions. This is understandable because the adults around them will have the child's safety in mind. They will also be concerned about social training and the constant effort required to keep the child attended to, on task, etc. and this can result in exhaustion for parents and carers. Very quickly the child can begin to build up a negative self-image. This in itself is possibly the most damaging influence on a child's personal and social development. As professionals we should not apportion blame. Chapter 3, on what the teacher can do, provides many inroads into increasing our understanding and encouragement of pupils to adopt good habits.

ADHD Occurence

Identification and diagnosis of ADHD is growing at an ever-increasing rate. Estimates of ADHD occurrence vary widely from 1% to over 11% of the population (Merrell and Tymms, 2001; NICE, 2000; Norwich *et al.*, 2002). Taking the average figure indicates one child in every class. The implications are that 90% of pupils with ADHD will under-achieve in school (Promoting Children's Mental Health within Early Years and School Settings, 2001). US data (Barkley, 1994) indicates over 20% of pupils with ADHD will be permanently excluded from school, over 35% may fail to complete high school, 20 to 30% have co-morbid learning disability, over 50% have significant social interaction problems with peers. We need to look at this significant portion of the population with increased understanding. ADHD is found at every IQ level, and the condition is more common in boys, in a ratio of about 4:1. There is some evidence that girls go relatively unidentified, as their behaviour is less overt, even though they may be at similar risk of learning and social difficulties.

2 | A History of the Development of the Definition of ADHD

The roots of the definition of ADHD arguably go back as far as Still (1902), who described a type of child having a 'defect of moral control'. Still drew up a list of qualities illustrating the condition: passionateness, spitefulness/cruelty, jealousy, lawlessness, dishonesty, wanton mischievousness/destructiveness, shamelessness/immodesty, sexual immorality and viciousness. Adding that:

> *'the keynote of these qualities is self-gratification ... without regard to the good of others or to the larger and more remote good of self. Some of these qualities ... are natural to children at a certain age and to a certain extent: it is their persistence in a degree unusual for the particular age and not corresponding to the influences of environment which constitutes their abnormality.' (p. 1009)*

The currently accepted diagnostic criteria began to develop in the *Diagnostic and Statistical Manual* (DSM) II (APA, 1968) where criteria attempted to differentiate ADHD from learning disabilities. DSM III (APA, 1980) states:

> *'in the past a variety of names have been attached to this disorder, including: Hyperkinetic Reaction of Childhood, Hyperkinetic Syndrome, Hyperactive Child Syndrome, Minimal Brain Damage, Minimal Brain Dysfunction, Minimal Cerebral Dysfunction, and Minor Cerebral Dysfunction.' (p. 41)*

DSM III (APA, 1980), DSM III-R (APA, 1987) and DSM IV (APA, 1994) have each added further refinements to the description of criteria for the diagnosis of ADHD, and the latest of these, DSM IV, indicates the possibility of ADHD being subdivided into three subtypes, these being: i) combined type, ii) predominantly inattentive type and iii) predominantly hyperactive/impulsive type (Merrell and Tymms, 2001). This has the label attention deficit hyperactivity disorder and is now used as an umbrella term for the three subtypes. The table below shows the development of the diagnostic criteria since 1980 to the currently used criteria of DSM IV (1994).

	DSM version			
	DSM III (1980)	DSM III-R (1987)	DSM IV (1994)	Observed trend
Title	Attention deficit disorder	Attention-deficit hyperactivity disorder (ADHD)	Attention-deficit/ hyperactivity disorder	Recognition of attention deficit with or without hyperactivity
Essential features	Signs of developmentally inappropriate inattention and impulsivity	Developmentally inappropriate degrees of inattention, impulsiveness and hyperactivity	Persistent pattern of inattention and/or hyperactivity-impulsivity that is more frequent and severe than typically observed in individuals at a comparable level of development	Consistent emphasis on developmentally inappropriate degrees of inattention, impulsiveness and hyperactivity
Subtypes	1. Attention deficit disorder with hyperactivity 2. Attention deficit disorder without hyperactivity 3. Residual type for those diagnosed with (1) but where hyperactivity is no longer present but other signs persist	No further clarification on subtypes	1. Attention-deficit/ hyperactivity disorder, combined type 2. Attention deficit/ hyperactivity disorder, predominantly inattentive type 3. Attention deficit/ hyperactivity disorder, predominantly hyperactive-impulsive type	No significant changes
Forms of disorder	DSM says it is not clear whether or not there are two forms of a single disorder	No further clarification		
Associated features	Vary as a function of age and include obstinacy, stubbornness, negativism, bossiness, bullying, increased mood lability, low frustration tolerance, temper outbursts, low self-esteem and lack of response to discipline	Vary as a function of age and include mood lability, low frustration tolerance, temper outbursts, low self-esteem. Academic underachievement is characteristic	Vary depending on age and developmental stage, may include low frustration tolerance, temper outbursts, bossiness, stubbornness, excessive and frequent insistence that requests be met, mood lability, demoralization, dysphoria, rejection by peers and poor self-esteem	
Comorbidity	Non localized 'soft' neurological signs and motor-perceptual dysfunctions (poor hand-eye co-ordination) may be present	Oppositional defiant disorder, conduct disorder and specific developmental disorders are often present. Functional encopresis and functional enuresis are sometimes seen. Non-localized 'soft' neurological signs and motor-perceptual dysfunctions (poor hand-eye co-ordination) may be present	Oppositional defiant disorder, conduct disorder. Mood disorders, anxiety disorders, learning disorders, communication disorders, Tourette's disorder	Consistently associated with oppositional defiant disorder and conduct disorder
Age at onset	Typically by the age of 3	Before the age of 4	DSM states it is difficult to establish diagnosis before the age of 4 or 5, but does allude to identification at earlier ages (2/3 years)	Recognized age of onset decreasing

| | DSM version | | | Observed trend |
	DSM III (1980)	DSM III-R (1987)	DSM IV (1994)	
Course	Three characteristic courses identified: 1. All symptoms persist into adolescent/adult life 2. All symptoms disappear at puberty 3. Hyperactivity disappears, but attention and impulsivity difficulties persist (residual type)	Disorder usually persists throughout childhood. Oppositional defiant disorder or conduct disorder often develop. Conduct disorder often develops into antisocial personality disorder in adulthood. Conduct disorder coupled with low IQ and severe mental disorder in parents predicts a poor course	Parents usually observe signs when child is a toddler. Diagnosis tends to be made in early school years. Tends to be relatively stable throughout adolescence/adulthood	Tends to be a persistent disorder
Impairment	Academic and social. Infrequently residential treatment may be needed	Social and school	Can be very impairing, affecting social/school/familial adjustment	Recognition of familial impairment as well as social/school
Predisposing factors	Mild/moderate mental retardation, epilepsy, some forms of cerebral palsy, and other neurological disorders	Central nervous sytem abnormalities i.e. neurotoxins, cerebral palsy, epilepsy, and other neurologic disorders. Disorganized/chaotic environments, child abuse/neglect		
Prevalence	Common, 3%	Common, 3%	3–5%	Increasing rate
Sex ratio	Ten times more common in male than female	Six to nine times more common in males than females	Male to female ratio ranging from 4:1 to 9:1	Recognition of condition in females increasing
Familial pattern	More common in family members than general population	More common in first degree biologic relatives than general population. Among family members specific developmental disorders, alcohol abuse, conduct disorder and antisocial personality disorder are overrepresented	More common in first degree biologic relatives. Higher prevalence of mood/anxiety disorders, learning disorders, substance-related disorders and antisocial personality disorder in family members	

Kewley (1999) has described ADHD as 'an internationally recognised medical condition of brain dysfunction, in which individuals have problems in inhibiting appropriate behaviour and controlling impulses, so giving rise to educational, behavioural and other difficulties' (p. 23). This description had previously been put forward by Anastopoulos *et al.* (1998); Cooper (1998a) and Taylor (1998). Kewley (1999) indicated that ADHD is frequently confused with other conditions, such as Asperger's syndrome, and with dyslexia, and can coexist with co-ordination and speech and language difficulties. Also he asserts that it often coexists with other mental health problems such as oppositional defiant disorder, conduct disorder, anxiety, depression and obsessive compulsive disorder.

There still remains much debate over whether or not ADHD is a discrete condition, part of another disorder, or a disorder at all. Riccio and Hynd (1996) examine the literature around central auditory processing disorder (CAPD) and ADHD, concluding that there is a difference between most ADHD cases and CAPD cases, thus strengthening the argument for a differential diagnosis. However Keller (1992) posited that the diagnosis of CAPD or ADHD depended on the evaluating professional's discipline, indicating the importance of a multidisciplinary approach to assessment and subsequent intervention as suggested by Riccio and Hynd (1996), while Hartmann (1999) suggests ADHD is an extreme personality type with useful attributes, rather than a disorder.

Literature exists (Barkley, 1990) to support the view that ADHD is a separate disorder found in adults and children, however the ADHD population has been found to overlap significantly with other disorders such as learning disorder and specific language disorder (Cantwell and Baker, 1991; Knivsberg *et al.*, 1999). Epstein *et al.* (1991) suggest that academic and social functioning will be impeded by poor attention, impulsivity and hyperactivity, thus being the possible cause for developmental learning disorders, rather than vice versa.

The American perspective chronicling the current state of the debate surrounding what is commonly called ADHD is studied by Rafalovich (2001). He examines this collection of symptoms from the psychodynamic and neurological perspectives in an attempt to define the phenomenon of ADHD. Since its so-called discovery, a century ago, several causes have been attributed to it, in addition to the neurological and psychodynamic previously discussed. Rafalovich (2001) cites *Encephalitis Lethargica*, premature birth, food additives and exposure to media imagery, as other possible causes that have contributed to the debate successively. In addition to this list can be added food intolerances, e.g. allergies to dairy and wheat, *Candida Albicans* sensitivity, and simply an extreme personality type, but not an illness or disease (Hartmann, 1999). However none of the above seems to be favoured as much as the neurological perspective. The psychodynamic perspective, which understands 'ADHD-like childhood behaviour as reactions to environmental conditions, rather than being specifically linked to organic causes' (Rafalovich, 2001, p. 399) has been largely overtaken by the neurological. Much of the success of this view must be attributed to the apparent success of medication in ameliorating the behaviours associated with ADHD, thus endorsing the argument that ADHD has a neurological basis (p. 404) coupled with claims that brain scans (magnetic resonance imaging and positron emission tomography) have shown brain abnormalities in ADHD children (p. 411). Psychodynamic treatments were found to lack long-term effect on people exhibiting minimal brain dysfunction, which has also contributed to the cause of neurology. A contrasting view is given by Cains (2000) who believed the evidence to be too thin to support a neurological basis for the condition.

The view that ADHD could be an organic condition that it is possible to minimize or maximize according to environmental conditions is similar to the views cited by Rafalovich (2001) of Greenacre and Bender in their works on organic brain disease. Rafalovich states:

'This discussion preserved the notion that these children suffered from an organic condition, but did not perceive this condition as the sole variable for a child's behavioural problems.' (p. 402)

Rafalovich summarizes discussions over the last seven or eight decades thus:

'ADHD was understood as: a) the results of unhealthy dynamics within key agents of socialization, primarily the family; b) the results of frustration due to some unnamable organic condition of the mind, which prevented normal functioning within conventional institutions; c) the behavioural results of a specific neurological process, traceable to neurotransmitters and regions of the brain.' (p. 414)

The ADHD debate still rages. The most useful perspective is possibly that all of the above are significant factors and the much talked about, but less often observed, multi modal approach (British Psychological Society 2000) to the management of ADHD would appear to be the best way forward, involving management strategies that help to minimize the negative side of this condition, rather than maximize them. It would seem that part of that multi modal approach is the management in school.

What does a child with ADHD look like?

At times the ADHD child is indistinguishable from any other child. This is where some of the misunderstanding of the condition arises. At other times the child will display some of the behaviours on the Teacher's checklist in Section 3 to a much greater degree than his peers.

It must be noted here that in general it is very clear to all those around that the child is having difficulties above those of her peers. ADHD is not usually something that needs to be searched for. The symptoms are usually only too plain to see. The adults around the child will often show signs of stress resulting from the excessive demands.

Children with ADHD may have difficulties with auditory processing even if their hearing is good. This can cause problems with following instructions. A child with ADHD will often feel confused about what they are expected to do. They are likely to suffer from repeated chastisement for their inattentive, impulsive and disruptive behaviour. Their self-esteem plummets and then a disaffected child may develop the additional oppositional defiant disorder characterized by argumentativeness, habitual non-compliance and lack of temper control (characterized by aggression, deceitfulness, rule-breaking activity and destructive behaviour) or s/he may grow into a disaffected teenager with conduct disorder.

ADHD is sometimes associated with other disorders, e.g. tic disorders or Tourette's syndrome, autistic spectrum disorders including Asperger's syndrome; obsessive compulsive disorder; emotional disorder; specific learning difficulties; speech and language; dyspraxia and hearing impairment, but frequently occurs without any of the above.

The diagnosis/identification debate

Do we really need to diagnose ADHD? The answer to this question is, in a perfect world, where everyone had ultimate patience and understanding, possibly 'no'. However the world is not perfect and help is sometimes required that cannot be accessed in any other way, i.e. medication. Nevertheless there are other ways to minimize the negative effects of ADHD, but they rely on:

1. early identification (pre-school if possible);
2. routine, consistency, behaviour guidance, praise for achievement of behavioural targets, all within a framework of loving discipline;
3. non-judgemental support for the family;
4. the child growing up in the knowledge that he is loved even though some of his behaviour may not be loved;
5. the child growing up in the knowledge that she has gifts and talents that if nurtured will enable her to function usefully and happily in adult society.

There is no suggestion here that simply applying good parenting practice and good teaching alone will work. ADHD in the home and classroom is a challenge to the best of parents and teachers and requires advanced positive parenting and teaching skills. The adults around the child must aim to channel the child's energy into positive and rewarding achievement. Any particular enthusiasm should be channelled and encouraged to positive effect.

None of the aspects above rely on a medical diagnosis, however a medical opinion is advisable if there are neurological damage concerns or if the problem appears to require medication as part of the therapy programme.

There is also a growing alternative therapy market making success claims, for instance homeopathy, dietary therapy, cranial osteopathy, thought pattern management, reflexology and massage may have their part to play in improving the lives of those affected. Availability of such therapies on the National Health Service is increasing, but is not yet likely to be the first option offered. As teachers we need to be aware that there are a number of ways ADHD children can be helped, and as well as playing our part in the therapeutic process by employing advanced teaching techniques, and ultimate patience, we need to encourage and support families in their search for help.

Seeking a medical opinion

Identification of ADHD type behaviour does not require a medical diagnosis, however the only sure way to acquire the label ADHD is to get a diagnosis by a clinician. Before seeking such a diagnosis consideration needs to be given to what benefit is expected in acquiring a diagnosis. For some the label ADHD is welcome, others are not so keen. Adolescent pupils can suffer cruel name calling in relation to their label. The label can on the other hand act as a soother for parent and child and indicate that the world has acknowledged their difficulties, however it can also be used as an excuse for the unwanted behaviour. A diagnosis can also act as a gateway to disability allowances. If conventional medication is what the parents and child wish to consider, then only a medical diagnosis will provide that. However, if dietary or behaviour management or homeopathy are the preferred choice, a good dietician, behaviour therapist specializing in ADHD, or a good homeopath, may be more useful. It is now possible to get a much wider range of treatments and therapies on the NHS than ever before. However, there could be a possibility that symptoms are caused by neurological damage such as head injuries, meningitis, encephalitis, brain haemorrhages and some types of epilepsy, in which case a medical referral is needed.

A catch-all would be to get a medical referral and ask for all treatment options for a child 'at risk of ADHD' or with 'significant ADHD type behaviour' to be discussed should treatment be deemed necessary. Once a label is applied it is sometimes hard to lose it.

It is important that the teacher does not put undue pressure on a family to go for a medical referral, but instead outline the options and let the parents decide. If parents do wish to have a referral the school or support services can refer the child. In many areas a referral does not have to be made by the GP.

How a diagnosis is made

When deciding on a diagnosis, clinicians generally refer to the *International Classification of Diseases* – 10th edition (ICD-10) and/or the *Diagnostic and Statistical Manual of Mental Disorders* – 4th edition (DSM-IV) criteria for diagnosis. Diagnosis criteria for ADHD are to be found in the DSM-IV produced by the American Psychiatric Association. Subtypes called predominantly inattentive (also know as ADD) and predominantly hyperactive-impulsive are also recognized.

Evidence will be gathered from a number of different settings. The school should be asked for a report on a child under investigation as the diagnostic criteria are required to be fulfilled in at least two settings. This report will be read in conjunction with a history from the parents or main carers.

Environmental factors

Although there are no particular causes or links to parenting, the environment is a major factor. ADHD can be maximized or minimized in differing situations. A family with a child who has severe ADHD can become stressed and dysfunctional, which can then exacerbate the child's problems. An ADHD child born into an already stressed and/or dysfunctional family may add to the dysfunction and will not receive the extra care and attention he needs. It is vital to consider all possible causes and secondary effects of ADHD when assessing and planning support systems. Successes with ADHD type children have been observed as follows: when living conditions allow for lots of noisy expression without being nagged at by neighbours or parents; when there are plenty of adults around to give the child an audience or reference point; when the child is surrounded by people who cherish and value his/her contribution to life; when there are plenty of constructive activities going on around the place for him/her to participate in; when the family are not ostracized by society for the behaviour of the child; when the child is not ostracized by the family for his/her behaviour; when the child is fed a healthy diet without lots of fizzy drinks, sweets and processed foods; when the living conditions are not overcrowded; when TV and computer gaming is limited; when there are set routines about getting up, going out, going to bed, mealtimes; when the child attends a school that is well disciplined and orderly; when both parents are living together and working well together, and are not mentally ill. This last point may sound a little glib, but in fact there are links between ADHD, mental illness and genetic factors. A significant number of young people suffering from ADHD type behaviour will have parents or relatives who are prone to drug/alcohol abuse and depression. Clearly if the child is living in a household already affected by these factors, the ADHD will put further strain on what is already a difficult situation. It is also possible that the ADHD type behaviour will be exacerbating the adult destructive behaviour in the house as it may be their only way to cope at the time. All of these factors need to be considered when supporting a family affected by ADHD.

Comorbidity

Comorbidity can be another source of confusion. This means the presence of two different conditions in the same child, or overlapping diagnoses. ADHD is particularly likely to overlap with other conditions.

In some cases it is not clear whether the other condition is responsible for the symptoms of ADHD, or vice versa, or whether some underlying condition is responsible for both. Whatever the direction of causality, it is important for the child's sake to diagnose all significant conditions. These may include: specific learning difficulties; autistic spectrum disorders; conduct disorder; oppositional defiant disorder; Tourette's disorder; obsessive compulsive disorder; depression; anxiety.

Early identification of ADHD is essential if disorders such as conduct disorder, oppositional defiant disorder, depression and anxiety are to be minimized later on.

Medication

The decision to use medication for ADHD must not be taken lightly. As with any drug there can be side effects. However, the research has shown that although medication is not a cure it can, for some children, provide a window of opportunity for advanced parenting and teaching skills to be put into practice and the formation of good habits to be implemented. It really depends on personal philosophy regarding drug taking. Many children inhale steroids on a daily basis for asthma – there are side effects, but the practice continues.

If after a thorough assessment, including reports from school and home, a child is diagnosed by a clinician as having ADHD the family may be offered medication as part of a programme of intervention. The benefits of medication include the opportunity for the child to experience good and acceptable behaviour and the approval which accompanies that. Metaphorically speaking it can be a leg up into the saddle, rather than chasing round and round in circles to mount an over-large horse.

Naturally parents are going to want to know what substances they are accepting for their child, and the child and the parents need to know of the side effects such substances may have.

The debate over the use of medication for ADHD is a lively one and both sides have some convincing arguments, however each case needs to be considered individually against a background of knowledge about the medication and the family's own philosophy surrounding drug use. Some people won't let any drug pass their lips, others make frequent recourse to the medicine cabinet. Deciding where you personally lie on that continuum may be a useful exercise.

There are two drugs commonly used to treat ADHD – Methylphenidate hydrochloride commonly know as Ritalin, and Dextroamphetamine, commonly known as Dexedrine. Both are stimulants, which at first may sound counterproductive, however they work, it is thought, by increasing the effect of the neurotransmitters in the brain. ADHD people appear to have a deficit of such substances, so a stimulant tops this up and helps rather than hinders it. As with any drug an initial trial gradually increasing the dosage is needed to assess suitability of the drug and necessary dosage. Drug holidays may also be suggested and can be useful to test if the drug is having any effect, or if it is still needed. Medication can last for some years, but should initially be viewed as a short-term intervention with frequent review to check effects. If effects are found to be negligible treatment should be stopped.

- *Methylphenidate – Ritalin*
  There is a large body of evidence to suggest that Ritalin is effective in reducing hyperactivity and increasing concentration in some children. Ritalin is related to amphetamine and is a controlled drug because of the possibility of abuse and dependence. Ritalin is a short-acting drug taking effect about half an hour after administration, peaking about one hour after taking and tailing off after four hours. Two or three doses a day are usually required, one in the middle of the day. Ritalin is not licensed for children under 6 years of age. Dosages range from 10 mg a day to a maximum of 60 mg. There are slow release forms of Ritalin that need only be taken once a day, Ritalin SR and Concerta being two forms.

- *Dextroamphetamine – Dexedrine*
  Dexedrine has a similar effect to Ritalin and may be used if children do not respond well to Ritalin. It is generally a second choice.

There are number of side effects that can be observed when using either of the above:

Loss of appetite and subsequent weight loss
This situation usually stabilizes after the first few months, but careful monitoring of calorie intake by parents/carers is advisable. Children need opportunity and encouragement to eat high calorie foods such as cereal or sandwiches at times when the drug is wearing off, as this is when they are likely to feel hungry, i.e. first thing in the morning before the first tablet and last thing at night.

Sleeplessness
Once asleep children will usually sleep well. Sometimes a sleeping tablet, Clondine, may be offered. Sometimes an extra dose of Ritalin reduces sleeplessness.

Less frequent side effects
These include nervousness, mood swings, any existent tics can be exaggerated, anxiety, headaches, dizziness, hallucinations, and initial bruising.

Growth, blood pressure and white blood cell count should be monitored as these can all be affected.

Contraindications
Some children may be less suitable for treatment with stimulants than others. If the child suffers from epilepsy, tics or anxiety, medication could increase the likelihood of these occurring.

- *Atomoxetine*
  This is a new medication. It need be taken only once a day, it is a selective norepinephrine reuptake inhibitor, but it is not clear exactly how it works! It is also claimed to have few or no side effects.

Monitoring of medication

After an initial trial period of about three months a follow-up appointment with the clinician will establish whether the drug is working or not. At this appointment it will be necessary for monitoring information from the school to be available to help in the assessment of the treatment and to outline behaviour modification programmes that have been put in place while the drug has been used. Side effects such as weight change, appetite and sleep pattern will be checked. The child's views about the effects and feelings about taking the tables need careful consideration. Some children do not like the feeling they get when taking the medication and this view needs to be listened to.

If the evidence on balance suggests the situation is improving medication should probably continue. If side effects outweigh any benefits an alternative treatment should be tried. It is likely that the situation once stabilized will be monitored six monthly or even yearly.

Medication and behavioural management

The National Institute for Clinical Excellence (NICE) published Guidance on the use of Methylphenidate for ADHD (2000). This report accepts the view that approximately 5% of school-aged children are likely to meet ADHD diagnostic criteria with 1% suffering from 'severe' ADHD with a current need for medication. It emphasizes the need for early diagnosis based on 'comprehensive assessment, conducted by a child/adolescent psychiatrist with expertise in ADHD, reports being drawn from child, parents and school'.

The NICE report recommends a multidisciplinary approach to the treatment of ADHD as a biopsychosocial issue, rather than a purely medical one. Less severely affected children with ADHD may be served better by cognitive-behavioural therapy, psychotherapy, family interventions and educational interventions.

Medication and behavioural management can complement each other. The medication tends to provide the window of opportunity within which the behavioural management can take place. It is quite possible that behaviour management, with consistent principles applied at school and home, which continues after medication has ceased could be a recipe for success that is more acceptable than a reliance purely on medication.

ADHD and homeopathy

Some medical practitioners are happy to prescribe homeopathic treatment for ADHD, and if they are not prepared themselves they can refer a client to a specialist who is. The referral needs to come from the general practitioner at the request of the parent/guardian. Homeopathic treatment works by the administration of a substance that will create the same symptom as that which you are trying to eradicate. Homeopathy tries to cure the individual of the problem by activating the body's own system of balance to rectify the area of the body out of balance. Very small doses are given, just enough to kick-start the body's own defences. It must be stressed that as with any treatment, behaviour modification programmes should be the first method tried, but homeopathy does work for about 75% of cases. It must also be remembered that, just as with conventional medicine, the correct treatment sometimes takes a while to ascertain.

For further reading – *Ritalin Free Kids* (1996) argues the case for homeopathic treatment and explains the philosophy behind homeopathy.

ADHD and diet

Recent research (Richardson 2001, pp. 18–24) claims a link between dietary deficiencies of highly unsaturated fatty acids of the omega-3 and omega-6 series and development of dyslexia, dyspraxia, ADHD and autism. Dietary supplements are available but should always be taken with advice from the general practitioner. Foods naturally containing beneficial oils are fish such as sardine and mackerel. Much more information on this aspect of ADHD can be gained by contacting the Hyperactive Children's Support Group (hacsg@hacsg.org.uk).

Other alternative therapies

Success claims have been made for therapies ranging from cranial osteopathy through aromatherapy, reflexology, Indian head massage to thought pattern management (a form of Neuro Linguistic

Programming). It must be remembered that ADHD is a very broad condition with each individual case differing from the next, consequently it is very likely that a therapy or strategy that works for one child will not work for another, or even that a strategy which works on one day will not work on the next. Management of ADHD requires creativity, a good understanding of the concept of ADHD, patience and consistency.

Neuro Linguistic Programming (NLP)

NLP is becoming a more and more popular method of addressing problems. NLP is based on studying people who do things excellently, looking at an individual's strategies for doing things and then educating the neurological connections to do things differently. NLP therapy acts quickly and is likely to have much to offer the ADHD child and adult in the from of repatterning old habits. Help can be sought for concentration, self-confidence, frustration, anger management, organization, etc. through NLP. For more information on this, email katespohrer@hotmail.com.

What the teacher can do

As mentioned earlier, ADHD type behaviour occurs in most children from time to time. There is no ADHD behaviour which is so bizarre that a teacher will not have come up against it at some time. We are used to dealing with pupils going off task, seeking frequent attention and reassurance, and being impulsive. Use the teacher's checklist to assess any pupils who you are concerned may have ADHD. If they achieve a low score the activities that follow in this book will help.

The problem with ADHD type pupils is that they will challenge even the best, most consistent and organized teacher, and they will do it relentlessly. Because of this we get tired of their behaviour and begin to lose sight of our good teaching methods. The school staff questions on the following pages are to help you to ask yourself candidly if you are considering these factors daily as you teach.

ADHD school staff questions

The following four sets of questions can be used by those who work with ADHD pupils in the school to aid reflection on practice. Reflect on each question thinking of your own classroom examples. Try to think of ways you do or could address the issues raised by the question. Where there are gaps in practice consider strategies that would suit both the child and the classroom. Reflecting on the questions will help you to do this.

Use the questions to help you to write targets and strategies for an individual education plan (IEP). Experiment with practice and go back to the questions at a later time looking for changes in your practice; review, amend and begin the cycle again. Remember, when working with ADHD children you need to set very small, easily achievable targets, which will be swiftly reviewed. An IEP for an ADHD child needs to be very dynamic, i.e. it needs to be frequently amended. Three monthly or termly reviews will rarely result in progress, fortnightly will have a better chance.

A. About the child

1. Have concentration and attention skills been discussed with the pupil?
2. Does the pupil have any system to monitor these behaviours?
3. Have accurate observations of concentration span been carried out?
4. Which tasks are of interest to the pupil?

5. Are these used to set achievable targets in a behaviour plan?
6. Does the time and nature of tasks affect the length of concentration span?
7. How is the pupil's level of concentration affected by the time and events of the day?
8. How is such an effect taken into account when planning tasks for the pupil?
9. If medication is used are dose times taken into account when planning tasks for the pupil?
10. What kinds of tasks does the pupil work best on? Can more of these be built into the curriculum?
11. Have hearing, sight and language checks been carried out recently to rule out problems in these areas?
12. What is your relationship with the pupil like? Do you take a genuine interest in the pupil? Do you take time to talk socially with him/her?
13. Do you run a 'Circle of Friends' type programme (Maines and Robinson, 1998) to help this child make and maintain friendships?
14. Is there a skill the child has that can be used to help the school community, thus developing responsibility and self-esteem?
15. Do you maintain your sense of humour at all times?!!?

B. Giving instructions

1. Do you ensure the pupil is looking at you before giving instructions?
2. How could you give the pupil a discrete cue to begin work?
3. Do you break work down into small amounts to tackle at a time?
4. Do you provide one instruction at a time in large print?
5. Do you provide prompts and signposts to help keep the pupil on task?
6. Do you explain the purpose of the work and how it is meant to look when it is finished?
7. Do you suggest an appropriate amount of time to be spent on each task?
8. Do you get the pupil to repeat the instructions back to you before commencing the task?
9. Do you follow the good listening code in your classroom, i.e. teach children to:
   - sit up straight and still
   - look at the speaker
   - think about what the speaker is saying
   and give positive behaviour specific feedback to those pupils complying with the code?
10. Do you ensure opportunities arise for controlled movement around the classroom?

C. Classroom organization/teaching styles

1. Have you audited which situations create less concentration and attention problems and which create more? How could you/do you do this?
2. Does the pupil work at a clear desk?
3. Does the pupil need to doodle or fiddle with an object while listening to the speaker?
4. Do you use good role models and peer mentors to work with the pupil in lessons?
5. Do you ensure the pupil is sitting away from distractions such as windows, switches, etc.?
6. Have you set clear parameters of appropriate behaviour, i.e. when it is appropriate to get out of his seat and when not?
7. Are you consistent in your enforcement of these parameters?
8. Do you allow the pupil to work in a special, quiet place?
9. Do you negotiate with him when he needs to make the choice to go to that special place?
10. Have you thought about using a sand timer to help the pupil time tasks?
11. What teaching style decreases the difficult behaviours?
12. Do you alternate short, independent tasks with longer, teacher-assisted tasks?
13. How are tasks differentiated according to learning style?
14. How do you gear work to ensure success will be gained?
15. What methods of assessment (other than written) are used?
16. How do you ensure seating arrangements enable the best chance of success for the pupil?
17. Do you ensure the pupil can see the whiteboard easily (without turning round)?
18. Do you use physical exercises on a regular basis throughout the day to aid concentration and attention?
19. Do you use relaxation techniques with your class at least once a day?
20. Do you start your lessons by focusing or centring, e.g. a few seconds concentrating on breathing?
21. Do you ensure that opportunities arise for controlled movement around the classroom?
22. Do you ensure that opportunities arise for the child to take responsibility, e.g. to deliver notes, do errands?
23. Do you ensure that you have outlined clearly the behaviour that is expected of the children in your classroom?
24. Do you take curriculum time explicitly to teach behaviour?
25. Do you model appropriate behaviour at all times when you are on view to your class?
26. Do you teach what type of voice to use in different situations and give feedback on practice sessions?
27. Do you consistently affirm the type of behaviour you want to see?
28. Do you always keep cool when the classroom temperature seems to be rising?

29. Do you get to know the pupils so that you are able to tap into their sense of humour?
30. Do you set realistically achievable amounts of homework?
31. Do you make sure you stick to routines in the classroom?
32. Do you always keep cool when faced with non-compliant behaviour, and calmly and slowly explain the choices available to the pupil?
33. Do you communicate that you are saddened by the non-compliant behaviour, but that you are not ruffled by it, and will take time to consider your response?
34. Do you always state fairly the consequences of an action?
35. Do you encourage the pupil to consider the effects of his actions without asking him why he did something (a question he can never answer anyway)?

D. The feedback the child receives

1. How do you give positive behaviour-specific feedback for:
   - good listening
   - concentration
   - attention?
2. What praise do you give for:
   - good listening
   - concentration
   - attention?
3. How do you ensure negative feedback/correction is given discreetly without a pupil audience?
4. Do you ensure that precise behaviour-related positive comments outweigh your negative comments by a 4:1 ratio?
5. Do you create a bespoke behaviour programme that checks very frequently if negotiated targets have been achieved?

Teacher's checklist

Use the checklist below to assess the pupil now, and again in six or nine months. Don't expect improvements quickly!

Agree a lot   1   2   3   4   Disagree a lot

Date		
Finds it hard to start work.		
Finds it difficult to listen to other people for more than a minute.		
Frequently loses his stuff.		
Finds it hard to get any work finished.		
Says things without thinking.		
Does things without thinking.		
Doesn't have many friends.		
Daydreams.		
Finds it really hard to sit still.		
Forgets instructions just after he has been given them.		
Anything going on in the room distracts him from his work.		
Slow at getting ready for PE.		
Interrupts other people's conversations.		
Hates to wait.		
Queues make him angry.		
Gets frustrated and upset when he can't do his work quickly.		
Likes to make friends but sometimes finds it difficult without help.		
Friendships don't last.		
Is sorry for things he's done wrong, then just does them again.		
Talks incessantly.		
Frequently out of his seat.		
Interferes with other pupils and property.		
Doesn't respond when concentrating on something he really enjoys.		
Can concentrate hard on things he likes doing.		
Asks lots of questions.		
Likes individual sport better than team games.		
Notices slight changes in the classroom.		
Has lots of energy.		
Has ideas that other people haven't thought of.		
Likes to be the leader when playing team games.		
Enjoys trying to solve problems.		

If the score is low this book should help.

Individual education plans

Every child with ADHD or ADHD-type behaviour is likely to warrant an individual education plan. The objective of such a plan is to help the school address the behaviour and learning, and to enable the child to get to know the way their mind works, so that they can have more control of their behaviour and eventually experience good life chances and contribute positively to society. A good IEP will be written in conjunction with the parents and the child, taking into account the child's view at all stages.

Two case studies follow. The first will exemplify how an IEP might be put together for an ADHD child. In the second comments and suggestions are made on the description given by a teacher of a child. These comments could be used to furnish an IEP.

Case study 1: Harry Hectic

Harry is a trial to his teachers. He is a whizz on computers, but his handwriting is described as atrocious, his written work output is very low and his teachers feel frustrated by this because they feel he has ability. Orally he is able to converse at an age appropriate or above level and can 'talk the hind legs off a donkey'.

His Mum reports she has always had difficulty with him behaviour wise, he was a poor sleeper and had to have medication to help him sleep as a young child. She also says he is always taking things, such as radios and speakers, apart, and putting them back together successfully.

Harry gets into a lot of trouble at school; he is always fiddling with something, tapping or quietly humming away to himself, but he has an ally in one of the teachers who believes he has a lot of talent if only it could be channelled. She works hard to persuade the other staff at the school that this is the case, but even she at times feels like giving up on him. Harry does not like art, finds spelling difficult and often loses his 'stuff'.

3

Individual education plan

Name: Harry Hectic   Class teacher: Mrs Smart   Year Group: 6
Date of birth: 01.01.200X   Preferred learning style: Active   Reading age: 9.2
Spelling age: 8.3
Start date: now   Review date: 3 weeks later
Interim review period: weekly with parents and Harry
Arrangements for monitoring IEP: SENCo will observe lessons at random

What targets are to be achieved? (Ensure they are small and achievable)	What strategies will be used?	Who will use these strategies?	How will the targets be monitored?	How will you know when targets have been achieved?	What support from home will help achieve targets?
1. Have my equipment in school: pen, pencil, ruler, rubber, in a pencil case	Leave pencil case in school at end of day	Class teacher to remind Harry at end of day when checking report card Member of peer group (chosen friend) to check with Harry	By report card completed lesson by lesson and checked at end of day for feedback with class teacher and weekly by SENCo	4 out of 5 days compliance	Parent to ensure Harry has duplicate equipment at home so he does not need to take his pencil case home
2. Do good sitting (sit up straight and still, look at the speaker, think about what the speaker is saying) for 50% of my time in lessons when required	Report card that registers Harry's sitting every 15 minutes (*Thus giving him a 'new life' every 15 mins*)	All who teach Harry	Report card will monitor pupil activity. SENCo will monitor implementation of programme	Negotiated rewards (computer time) will be awarded to Harry when he is working towards his target, and has reached his target (*E.g. each day when he has done 25% good sitting he receives a small reward, 50% earns him a larger reward. A cumulative larger reward, say a certificate from the head, at the end of the week could be a further incentive*)	Parents will feed back at weekly meeting with class teacher, Harry and SENCo
3. Encourage responsiblity	Harry to act as IT monitor for the class – ensuring computers switched off at end of day and helping people out when they are stuck, after permission given by teacher. (*This will also give him a legitimate reason to leave his chair and raise his status within the group*)	All who teach Harry	At weekly feedback sessions	When sense of responsibility can be transferred to other areas of school (*This may be a very long-term objective*)	Harry to be given a small responsibility in the family home to compliment his growing sense of responsibility at school (*This will help Harry to feel people trust him in more than one area of his life – very important for self-esteem to feel that we are trusted to make decisions*)

IEP drawn up collaboratively by:

SENCo	yes/no
Class teacher	yes/no
Subject teachers	yes/no
Advisory teacher/educational psychologist	yes/no
Pupil support unit co-ordinator	yes/no
Pupil	yes/no

IEP monitored by _____ on (dates) _____

This IEP could be slightly amended each week with 50% increasing to 60% and rewards being changed slightly to maintain the interest of the child. Harry likes computer time, but some children may respond better to having a corner of the room with some art equipment where they can go as a reward. I have seen this 'art station' idea used not simply as a reward but as part of the child's 'therapeutic curriculum'. The aim for these two targets would be to move Harry to being able to do good sitting for a majority of the time when required, 80% would be a satisfactory achievement, and to be able to remember to leave his pencil case at school ready for the next day without being reminded by friends or teachers. The key is to take it slowly, and to build in plenty of success for the child and, ultimately, for yourself. It is assumed that normal strategies regarding positive teaching, one negative to four positive comments, and ignoring as much trivial attention-seeking behaviour as possible while noticing and affirming appropriate behaviour with positive behaviour specific feedback, i.e. naming the behaviour you are pleased to see, will be a part of every classroom without having to be specifically mentioned on the IEP. Notice in this IEP there is no mention of 'stop tapping, making noises, etc.' Human beings find it very difficult to conceptualize the negative, so targets wherever possible need to be couched in terms of what we do want children to do. We want Harry to sit well and listen. If he is doing good sitting, i.e. he is sitting up straight and still and looking at the speaker, there is a good chance that he will be thinking about some of what the speaker is saying, and a reduced chance of him making noises and tapping fingers. Notice the target is for 50% of the time when required. Harry can have bonus points when the lesson doesn't require good sitting. We are not expecting angel wing buds to sprout!

Case Study 2: Hetti Hectic

Teacher: Hetti is a constant fidget and talker in class. She is described as having average to above average ability, but a problem in reaching what the school considers to be her potential, particularly where pen and paper tasks are involved.

Hetti may be able to indicate her true ability if she were given more opportunities to feed back what she knows in a form other than pen and paper, for example using a PC, tape recorder, working with a group of other children who record what she is saying, or orally with teacher or support staff.

Teacher: It has been noticed that she can apply herself to work quite quickly if she is kept in after the bell.

Don't get drawn into the 'she can do it when she chooses to' trap. Hetti may find she needs an extra stimulus to help her to concentrate on the task in hand. She may respond well to having a kitchen timer or sand timer to help her complete work in set times.

Teacher: Hetti took part in a project where relaxation exercises were practised regularly each week. It was noticed that during these sessions she found it impossible to keep still, 'there was always a little rustling or chinking of change when Hetti was with us'.

Keep trying on this one, it will pay off in the end, but don't be too ambitious with the time she is expected to keep still for, start with a few seconds and gradually build up. She needs to experience peace and quiet, and that will be hard for her at first.

Teacher: Hetti is the type of child who while walking across the classroom flicks, prods or play kicks other children.

A behaviour programme targeting interfering with other children could be a start here. Frequent monitoring and feedback are essential for success. Frequent means acknowledgement every 15 minutes that she is doing OK, with rewards built in when she has done well for 5, 10, 15, 20 and 25 sessions. This should be cumulative, not consecutive, to ensure she gets a new life every 15 minutes. Rewards should be the minimum that will work. This sounds labour intensive, but if applied diligently for a short period of time it should produce some success upon which to build.

Teacher: Naturally other children find this tiresome, so her popularity wavers.

A friends support group (e.g. Circle of Friends as described in All for Alex*) could help Hetti with her relationships. It could also help other children to understand some of the difficulties Hetti has in controlling her actions, they will then be able to prompt and remind her when she is beginning to veer off course.*

Key points for writing an IEP for an ADHD child:

- Ascertain the child's strengths, and build on them.
- Know the child's preferred learning style.
- Know about some of the things the child is interested in outside school – these could be used as motivators, showing interest in them will also help your relationship with the child.
- Find out from the child the behaviour that causes them trouble in the classroom which he/she thinks would be easiest to change – always work on this one first as you want to get success to build on.
- Set appropriate targets which are not so hard that they set the child up to fail.
- If a target is looking a bit sticky, have a rest from it, you can always return to it later, but make sure the child knows the plan as well as you.
- Monitor consistently and frequently; preferably use a programme that gives regular – several times a lesson – positive behaviour specific feedback.
- Review frequently with parents, child and interested teachers.
- Change rewards frequently – even best quality ice cream with your favourite topping loses its appeal after a while.
- Approach IEP writing from a team problem-solving perspective – the team includes teachers, parents and child.
- Think about how the behaviour makes you feel and what the child is communicating by that – remember that human beings transfer feelings to each other, so if the child is making you feel anxious in the classroom it is most likely they have been experiencing that feeling too; now they are passing it to you to cope with.
- Always maintain your sense of humour, but never use jokes to belittle a child; help them to laugh at themselves by being able to laugh at yourself.
- Use the ADHD school staff questions to prompt reflective practice and give ideas for strategies.

Individual Education Plan

Name: Class teacher: Year Group:

Date of birth: Preferred learning style:

Reading age: Spelling age:

Start date: Review date: Interim review period:

Arrangements for monitoring IEP:

What targets are to be achieved? (Ensure they are small and achievable)	What strategies will be used?	Who will use these strategies?	How will the targets be monitored?	How will you know when targets have been achieved?	What support from home will help achieve targets?
1.					
2.					
3.					

IEP drawn up collaboratively by
SENCo   yes/no
Class teacher   yes/no
Subject teachers   yes/no
Advisory teacher/educational psychologist   yes/no
Pupil support unit/co-ordinator   yes/no
Pupil   yes/no
IEP monitored by _____ on (dates) _____

Supporting Children   **29**

Part 2: Pupil activities and exercises

4 | Self-esteem

Letter to the child

Hello,

My name is Kate Spohrer. I am a teacher who works with children who have ADHD or concentration and attention difficulties. I have also lived with people who have ADHD, so I know some of the problems.

I hope that this book will help you to understand that you are not alone. There are loads of people like you, and there are lots of things you can do to make your life a little bit easier.

I hope you enjoy this book. When you have tried some of the things suggested in here, will you get in touch with me? I would love to hear from you. You can email me on katespohrer@hotmail.com

Give it a try and get in touch!

Good luck,
Kate. E. Spohrer

ADHD – What does this mean?

So, you have been identified as having Attention Deficit Hyperactivity Disorder. What does this mean?

There are lots of different types of people. Some of those types are very slow and like to do the same thing over and over again, others like to do things quickly and like to do lots of different things. The picture below shows how most people are a bit of both.

But some people are right at the ends of the curve. You happen to be somewhere around here.

This needn't be a problem, but it could be if you don't get to know yourself and how *your* brain works.

If you are at the ADHD end of the curve you are likely to be easily distracted from anything you try to do. If you are like me you'll walk across the room to fetch something and return 30 seconds later having forgotten what you went for.

You could be a fidget, or hyperactive, especially when you are expected to listen to someone talking. You might keep changing position on your seat, sitting on your feet or lolling. This is all because you find it hard to keep awake in situations like that. You could be inattentive, maybe you like to doodle. I had to doodle through all my lectures at college. I thought of getting a pair of glasses with pictures of eyes on so I could go to sleep unnoticed!

You may be impulsive – that means you could say things you later wished you hadn't. Do you know that feeling?

You may not have all of these characteristics, or you may have some of them more in some situations than others. As I said, you need to know yourself, then you can work round your difficulties and use your strengths to best effect.

Pupil's checklist

Name:

Look at the descriptions below and mark those things you think describe you.

Date	Agree a lot		Disagree a lot	
	1	2	3	4
It's hard for me to start my work.				
I find it difficult to listen to other people for more than a minute.				
I lose my stuff.				
It's hard for me to get any work finished.				
I say things without thinking.				
I do things without thinking.				
I don't have many friends.				
When I should be concentrating on my work I think about other things.				
I find it really hard to sit still.				
I find that just after I have been given instructions I forget them.				
Anything going on in the room takes my attention away from my work.				
I am slow at getting ready for school.				
I can't help butting in to other people's conversations.				
I hate to wait.				
Queues make me angry.				

Always hold on to this thought –

THERE ARE A LOT OF THINGS I AM BETTER AT THAN LOTS OF OTHER PEOPLE.

I get frustrated and upset when I can't do my work quickly.				
I like to make friends but sometimes find it difficult without help.				
I am sorry for things I've done wrong, but I do them again without thinking.				
I can concentrate hard on things I like doing.				
People think I can't hear properly when I'm concentrating on something I really enjoy doing.				
I ask lots of questions.				
I like individual sport better than team games.				
I notice slight changes in my classroom.				
I have lots of energy.				
I have ideas that other people haven't thought of.				
When I am playing team games I like to be the leader.				
I enjoy trying to solve problems.				

Now that you have thought about these things you can plan how to help yourself.

About your brain

Your brain controls your behaviour.

In the brain there are chemicals called neurotransmitters whose job it is to carry messages from one brain cell to another, just like a car or a bus carries passengers. Imagine if all the fuel in the filling stations dried up. We would not be able to get around. The neurotransmitters are like the cars and buses that move us around. In your brain's case it is messages that are moved.

What do you think would happen if we could not get around? Would we all get to work and to school, or would we all be stuck at home unable to get to the shops to buy food and all of the other things we need? That's a little bit like the situation in the brain of someone with ADHD. Sometimes there aren't enough neurotransmitters to make sure messages move from one part of the brain to the other. But maybe your brain isn't meant to use a car and bus transport system. Maybe it's meant to be different.

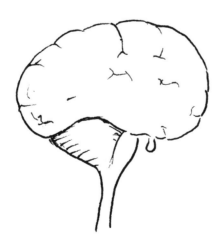

ADHD has a purpose

If you have ADHD you may find it brings with it many advantages. People with ADHD are often good look-outs because they are so good at noticing everything that's going on around them. They make good emergency workers like paramedics.

ADHD tends to run in families. If you think of your relatives you might be able to recognize members of your family who are a bit like yourself.

Jot down any members of your family you think you may be like. You might want to discuss this with your parents, sometimes they can tell you about what they were like when they were young, or what their brothers and sisters were like.

1.

2.

3.

4.

Food and drink

Food and drink affects everyone's behaviour, but if you have ADHD you need to be particularly careful about what you eat. Some people with ADHD have allergies or are sensitive to some foods and drinks. This results in them having less control of their behaviour when they have been eating or drinking them.

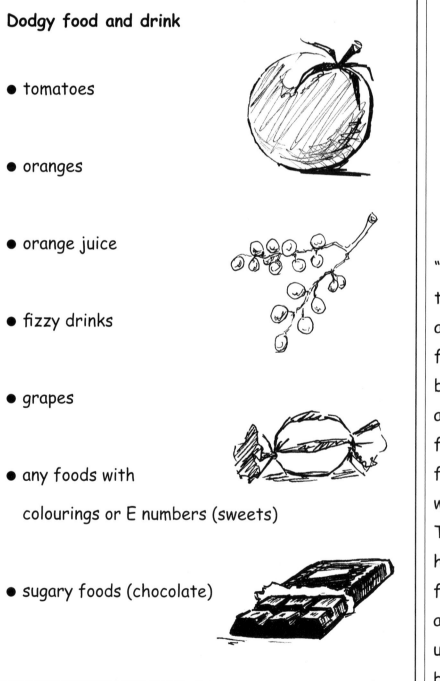

Dodgy food and drink

● tomatoes

● oranges

● orange juice

● fizzy drinks

● grapes

● any foods with

colourings or E numbers (sweets)

● sugary foods (chocolate)

"Oh no!" you're thinking those are some of my favourites. Your body can become addicted to these foods and you feel you can't do without them. Then when you have some you feel better – for a little while, until the bad behaviour starts.

What could you eat or drink instead?

-
-
-
-

Good food & drink	I like
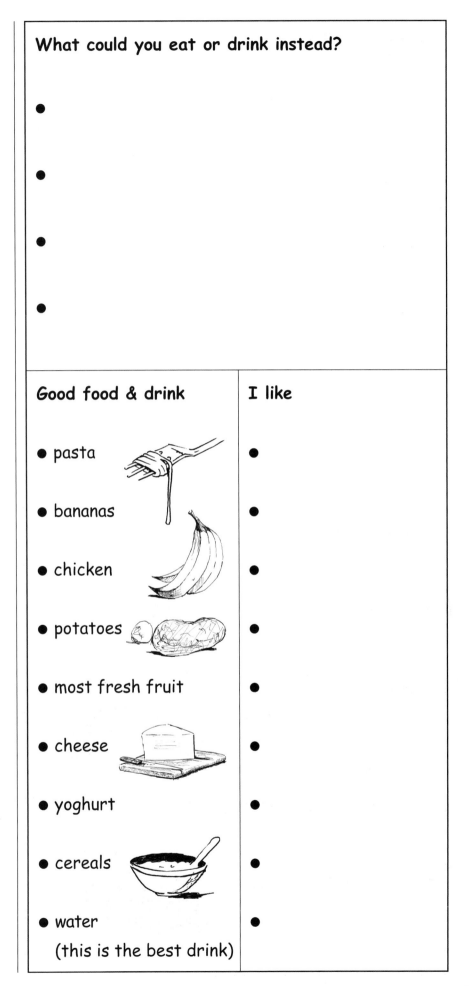	
● pasta	●
● bananas	●
● chicken	●
● potatoes	●
● most fresh fruit	●
● cheese	●
● yoghurt	●
● cereals	●
● water (this is the best drink)	●

If you are taking tablets for your ADHD you might find they take away your appetite. Try to eat at the times you are hungry, such as when the medicine is wearing off late at night, and before you take your first tablet in the morning. A bowl of cereal at night can be a good idea.

Can you plan a menu? Remember which foods are good for you.

Breakfast

Lunch

Dinner

Supper

Snacks

Are there any foods in that list that might be giving you a bad reaction, or that contain a lot of sugar or E numbers? Have a look on labels to see what's in food before you eat it. Your body is very precious so look after it.

Food	Ingredients
1. Ice cream	
2. Baked beans	
3. Tomato ketchup	

Self-awareness

About myself

The trouble with having ADHD is that it can be very hard to concentrate on some things. Even though you may be a really intelligent person some people might call you a scatterbrain because you forget about things and lose things. This annoys other people and sometimes they can be really hurtful to you and make you feel bad about yourself when you feel you can't help it.

Help is here. You can do something to train your brain – but you have to want to do it.

Describe yourself by filling in these statements.

My name is _____ .

I am _____ years _____ months old.

I am _____ cm tall.

My eyes are _____ .

I am _____ kg in weight.

My hair is _____ .

I have _____ brothers and _____ sisters.

Their names are

_____

_____

_____ .

I live with

_____

_____

_____

_____ .

I live at

_____

_____

_____ Postcode _____

Telephone number _____ .

Email address _____ .

This is me:

Would you rather...

- Have a bath in treacle OR mud?

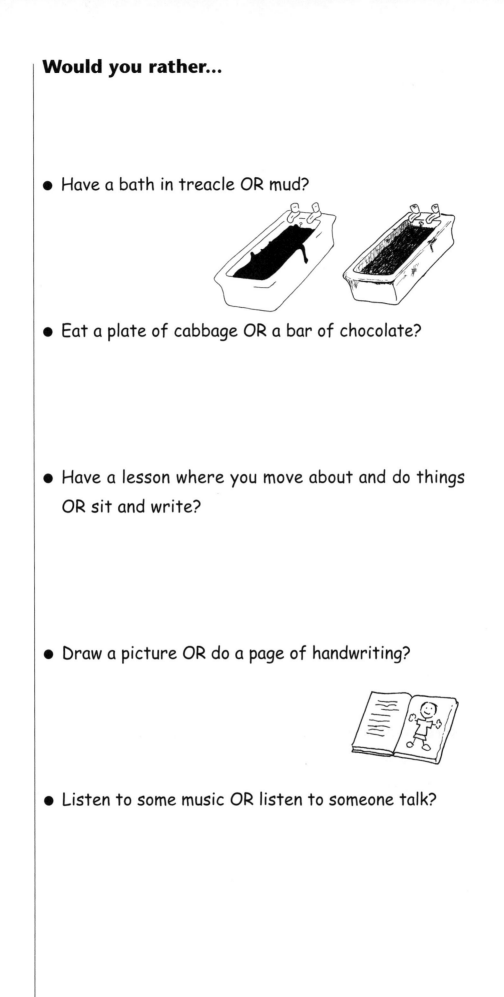

- Eat a plate of cabbage OR a bar of chocolate?

- Have a lesson where you move about and do things OR sit and write?

5

- Draw a picture OR do a page of handwriting?

- Listen to some music OR listen to someone talk?

- Tell jokes OR tell stories?

- Do some maths OR play football?

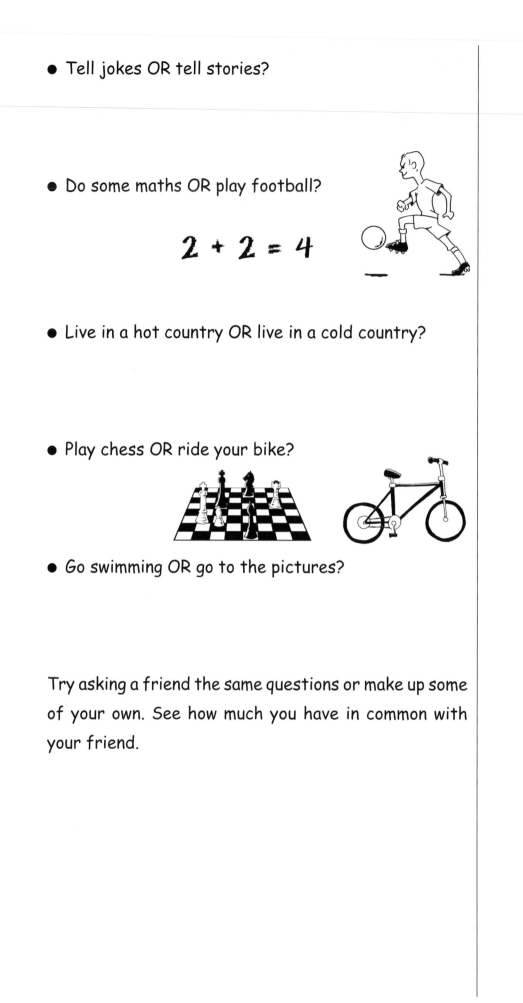

$$2 + 2 = 4$$

- Live in a hot country OR live in a cold country?

- Play chess OR ride your bike?

- Go swimming OR go to the pictures?

Try asking a friend the same questions or make up some of your own. See how much you have in common with your friend.

Your interview with a magazine journalist

Imagine news has got round that you are a very interesting person (because you are). A national magazine is sending their top journalist out to interview you. They are interested in finding out all about you and have sent a sheet of questions for you to think about before they see you.

What is your favourite game?

What is the best film you've ever seen?

What is the best book you've ever read?

What is your favourite music?

5

What is your favourite TV programme?

What do you concentrate best on?

When you are in the classroom, where are you sitting when you get on best with your work?

5

Who are the people who understand you most?

Why do you think they understand you? What do they do to make you feel they understand you?

Do you like to do anything when you are trying to listen to people, for example doodle?

What helps you to remember instructions you are given?

What are you very good at?

What are your favourite subjects?

Have you got a least favourite subject?

Would you like to get better at anything?

What have you got better at lately?

Thank you for thinking about these questions. If there are any that you were not able to answer today keep them in the back of your mind and return to them when you have an answer.

5

Affirmations

It might sound silly, but telling yourself that you are good at things makes you get better at them. It's all about believing in yourself. Have a go.

Cut out these cards. Choose a different one each day and say it to yourself in front of the mirror each morning and in the evening before bed. Try to repeat it in your head throughout the day.

Every day I feel happier, healthier and calmer.

I am accurate and quick.

I am happy and good.

I am alert and a good listener.

I am confident.

I am still and peaceful.

5

I am helpful.

I am successful.

I am kind and considerate.

I am good and lovable.

I am polite and kind.

I am a good friend.

I am patient and careful.

I can laugh at myself.

I am persistent and determined.

I am organized and plan my time.

5

A perfect day

My perfect day would begin with...

After breakfast I would...

At school I would go to my favourite lessons...

At lunchtime I would play with...

5

In the afternoon my class would...

When I got home I would...

5

For tea I would have...

Before bed I would...

I am good at

Now fill in these 'I am good at' statements.

1. I am good at   *cleaning my shoes.*

2. I am good at

3. I am good at

4. I am good at

5. I am good at

6. I am good at

7. I am good at

8. I am good at

Friends

Friends

Friends are important for all sorts of reasons.
They can:

- help you out when you have a problem,
- share in a special moment,
- listen to your jokes,
- visit places with you, or
- think of good ideas with you.

Can you think of some other reasons for having a friend?

-
-
-
-
-
-

Making friends

Having ADHD can make it difficult to make and keep friends. Friends may sometimes find your energy and enthusiasm just too much so they need to have a rest from you.

This doesn't mean they don't like you, only that they get tired more quickly than you. Sometimes they can say and do nasty things because they are tired, and sometimes they wish they hadn't said or done those things.

You can practise making friends. You need to think about things you like to do, and of someone you know who you would like to do these things with.

For example:

I like James, together we could climb trees.

6

Now you do it.

I like _____ ,

together we could _____ .

I like _____ ,

together we could _____ .

I like _____ ,

together we could _____ .

I like _____ ,

together we could _____ .

Are you able to spend time with the friends you have mentioned above?

If not, talk to an adult to get help in arranging a favourite activity.

Being a good friend

Being a good friend means being able to give and take, being able to take turns, and being able to laugh at yourself. This is very important.

A good sense of humour is important. Many people with ADHD have a very good sense of humour. They love to laugh, to make jokes and fool around, but sometimes in the wrong place and at the wrong time. Having a good sense of humour is one of the greatest personality gifts you can have. Being able to laugh at yourself is another great gift. If you can laugh when things are getting you down you will soon be feeling better.

Look back over the last week and try to think of a time when you were able to see the funny side of something you did. Maybe you did something you were a bit embarrassed about but you were able to laugh about it.

Write down or tell your friend or teacher what happened. Remember you are thinking about seeing the funny side of your own behaviour.

6

This is what Darren told his friend:

"Last week I had to play a duet on the clarinet in a concert my music teacher was putting on with her pupils. I had been practising and was quite good at home. When it was time to start I positioned my fingers and started to blow. My partner played well, but I started to squeak and lose my timing. I felt like the comedy act and couldn't wait to get off stage. At the time it was awful, but on the way home my mum, dad and I couldn't stop laughing at how funny it was."

Other people's games

Sometimes you will need to play games chosen by someone else. Games usually require you to take turns and keep to some simple rules.

Try playing some games with a friend. Cards are great for this.

Can you think of other games you can play? (Here are some ideas – board games such as Snakes and Ladders or Scrabble, card games like Snap and Rummy, or dice games like Yahtzee.) Describe one to your friend. Remember to tell him the rules. Now play it together.

Rules are important so that everyone knows what is expected of them in the game. When you have learnt to take turns with one other person try playing with two or more people.

6

Making up your own games

It can be fun to make up your own games, but before you start you all need to know the rules. If you don't everyone gets muddled and upset because they don't understand.

Think of a game you and some friends have made up. What were the rules?

1.

2.

3.

4.

Did you sort the rules out first before you started to play properly?

Sometimes people with ADHD get described as bossy by their friends. That's because there are so many ideas rushing round in your head all at the same time that they come out in a rush without you being able to persuade people that they are good ideas.

Try slowing down and saying one thing at a time.

What do you like about your friends?

Think about your friends. What do you like about them?

-
-
-
-
-
-
-

6

What makes a perfect friend?

Describe your perfect friend.

6

7 | Organization and concentration

Slowing down

Sometimes you might be rushing around too fast. What can happen when you do?

You might...

- fall over.

- forget to dress properly.

- drop things.

- not have time to think up good ideas.

- knock things over.

- leave your PE kit in the bedroom.

- rush out of the lesson before taking down your homework.

- not read instructions properly.

Can you think of any more?

-
-
-

Learning to slow down

Have you got loads of ideas? Do you think that the rest of the world can't keep up with you? Are you afraid that if you don't blurt them all out now you'll forget them?

Try this:

Instead of blurting them all out scribble them down - write or draw - on a piece of paper. When I'm teaching I use my whiteboard for this. At home I use my fridge door like a whiteboard, or my diary - everything goes in that.

Sometimes it's really hard to remember things we need to do. One easy way is to write a list.

Make a list in words or pictures of all the things you want to do today. Here's an example of mine:

1) Have a bath

2) Ring my friend Sunita

3) Clean the kitchen floor

7

My to do today list

Now it's your turn.

My to do today list

1. _____

2. _____

3. _____

4. _____

5. _____

6. _____

7

Knowing what needs to be done is half the battle. What you need to do now is put them in order of priority. What is most important? Put that at the top of the list. Now decide *when* you are going to do all the things on your list. This is called scheduling.

Now you try:

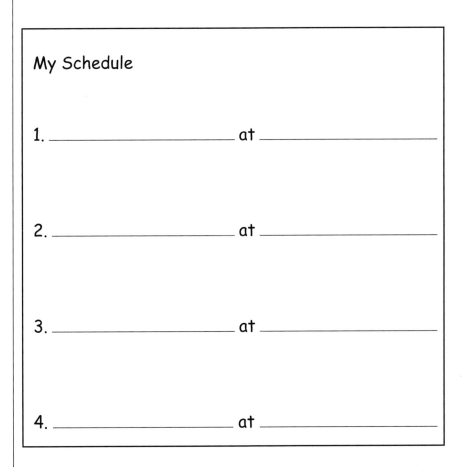

My Schedule

1. _____ at _____

2. _____ at _____

3. _____ at _____

4. _____ at _____

Things to carry over to tomorrow

Sometimes things need to be carried over to the next day. If you write down what they are you are less likely to forget them.

My to do tomorrow list

1. _____

2. _____

3. _____

7

I write lists for everything, and sometimes I cheat a bit by putting something on the list I've already done! It helps me feel I'm making progress. I break things down into little bits too. For example if I had some work to do, say some English homework in 3 sections a, b and c, my list would be:

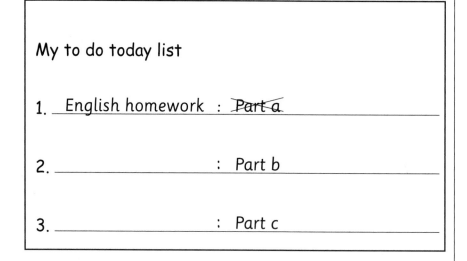

My to do today list

1. English homework : Part a _____

2. _____ : Part b _____

3. _____ : Part c _____

As soon as I'd done part 'a', I'd cross it off.

My to do today list

1. English homework : ~~Part a~~ _____

2. _____ : Part b _____

3. _____ : Part c _____

There, that feels much better. Before long you are ready to cross off part b and part c too.

7

Things you can do to help you concentrate

A few simple activities can really help your brain to work well.

Try this. Read out the letters of the alphabet, but each one has a coded instruction with it. So, when you read 'A', you must bend your knees. Practise going faster and slower – see the key.

A _B_	**B** _N_	**C** _S_	**D** _B_
E _S_	**F** _N_	**G** _S_	**H** _B_
I _N_	**J** _B_	**K** _N_	**L** _S_
M _N_	**N** _S_	**O** _B_	**P** _B_
Q _S_	**R** _N_	**S** _B_	**T** _N_
U _S_	**V** _N_	**W** _S_	**XYZ** _B_

Key

B = Bend your knees

N = Touch your nose

S = Stretch up with both arms

7

Yoga

This is a yoga posture. Yoga is really good for helping you to concentrate.

It is called 'Tadasana', which means 'the mountain'.

1. Stand with your feet hip width apart and heels and toes parallel.

2. Roll your shoulders gently to relax them.

3. Let your arms hang loosely by your sides.

4. Imagine there is a piece of string attached to the top of your head and it is gently pulling you up, gently stretching out your back bone. You should be a little taller now.

5. Keep your shoulders back and relaxed, with your arms hanging by your sides.

6. Now try to stand still for a few seconds, close your eyes if you can.

This can be very relaxing.

For lots more yoga look at a book called *Yoga for Children* by Mary Stewart and Kathy Phillips.

7

Making your own relaxation tape

You can make your own relaxation tape to help you relax when you are feeling tense. Read the script below slowly into the microphone on your tape recorder.

You will need:

- A tape recorder
- A tape
- This script
- A quiet place
- Some of your favourite relaxing music

Script

Sit comfortably in the chair.

Make sure both feet are flat on the floor.

Make sure your bottom is well back on the seat of the chair.

Make sure your back is straight.

Check you are looking straight ahead of you.

Now close your eyes.

Place one hand on your chest and one on your tummy.

Take three slow breaths.

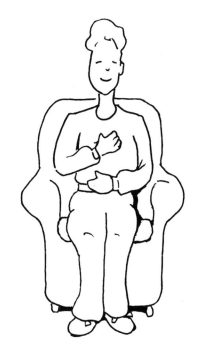

In ... out

In ... out

In ... out

Check which hand is moving the most.

Put the other hand back in your lap.

Take three more slow breaths.

In ... out

In ... out

In ... out

Place the other hand in your lap.

Keep your breathing slow.

Think about your toes.

Scrunch them up tight as you breathe in.

Hold for a breath out and in.

Let them relax on your next out breath.

Think about your legs.

Tighten the muscles in your legs as you breathe in.

Hold for a breath out and in.

Let them relax on your next out breath.

Think about the muscles around the base of your spine.

Tighten those muscles.

Hold for a breath out and in.

Let them relax on your next out breath.

Think about your chest and upper back.

Tighten those muscles.

Hold for a breath out and in.

Let them relax on your next out breath.

Think about your arms and hands.

Tighten those muscles, make fists with your hands.

Hold for a breath out and in.

Let them relax on your next out breath.

Think about your neck and face.

Tighten those muscles, make a really ugly face, stick your tongue right out.

Hold for a breath out and in.

Let them relax on your next out breath.

Now you have worked right through your body, you can tell the difference between tense and relaxed.

Scan your whole body to check for tense parts and relax them down as you breathe out.

Let go of tensions and thoughts.

Breathe slowly for five breaths trying to stay relaxed.

In ... out

In ... out

In ... out

In ... out

In ... out

7

Rub your hands together.
Place them over your eyes.
Open your fingers slightly.
Open your eyes.
Gradually open your fingers a little more.
Slide your hands down your cheeks bringing them to rest in your lap.

How do you feel?

You might like to add some of your favourite relaxing music at the end of this tape.

7

Puzzles

Puzzles like 'spot the difference' can help you to slow down and concentrate on your work. Try finding the nine differences in the puzzles below.

It's good to practise this kind of exercise. See if you can find any more books with puzzles like this in. There are usually a few at the local newsagents.

Sequencing

Sometimes you might want to do so many things all at the same time that you get confused as to what order to do them in. Knowing what order to do things in is called sequencing. If you are the type of person who only thinks about putting a raincoat on after you are soaked, maybe you should practise sequencing.

Put these pictures in order by writing the numbers 1–4 in the boxes below them.

Need a harder one? Ask your teacher.

Supporting Children

Following instructions

It is important to read all the instructions before you start.

Follow the instructions below.

1. Write your name at the top of this box.
2. Underline your name in pencil.
3. Draw a picture of a man and/or woman in space a).

a)

4. Complete only instruction 1 in this box.

Did you follow all of the instructions? It is important to read all the instructions first.

7

Writing your own instructions

Can you write a set of instructions for making beans on toast?

Or a set of directions between your classroom and the library?

●

●

●

●

●

Ask your friend to follow the instructions. Did they work?

7

Circle pictures

Now try this.

Making pictures and patterns inside a circle is a very calming thing to do. It will help your thoughts to come in a more ordered way.

In the circles, fill in your own patterns or pictures.

7

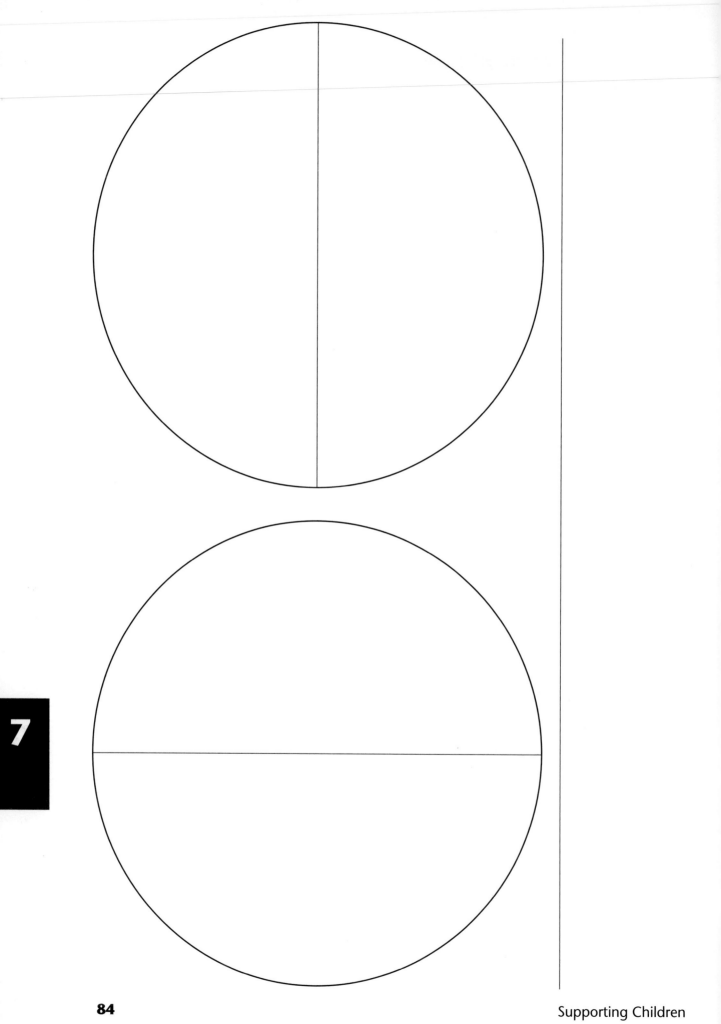

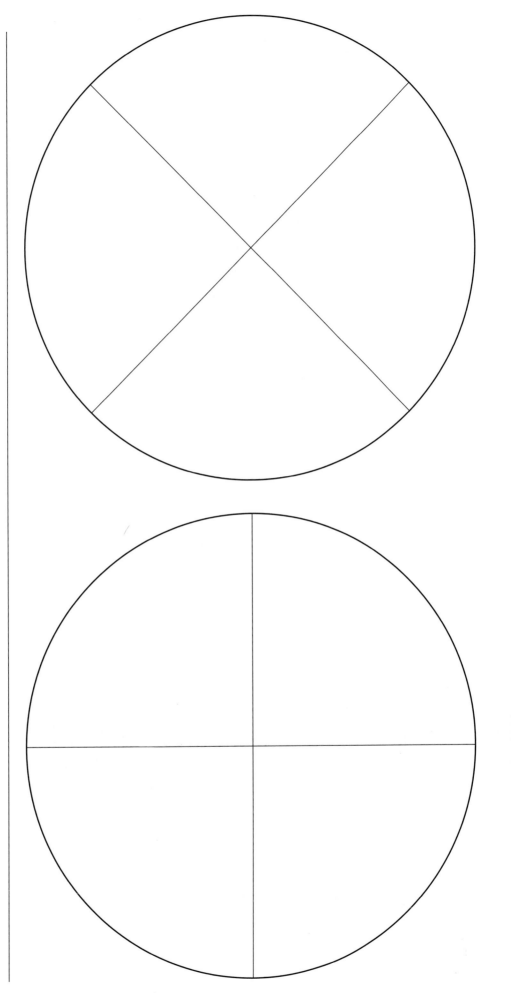

7

Here are some ideas of patterns you can make using compasses.

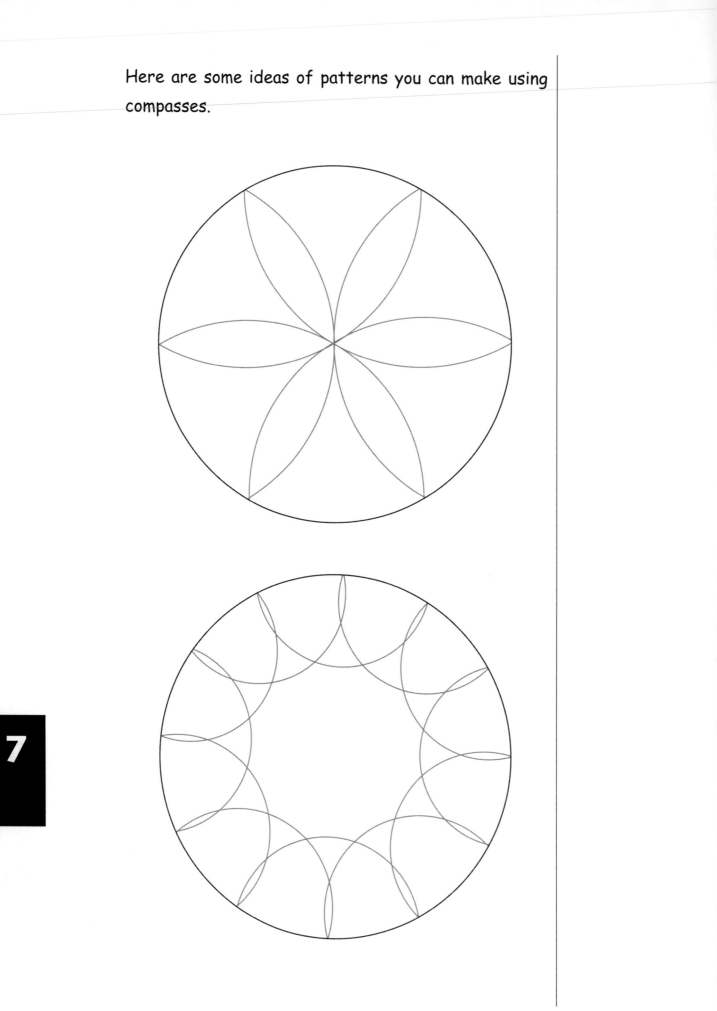

Time management

Here are some hints on how to manage your time well

1. Slow down and work carefully.

2. Break jobs down into small parts.

3. Make a plan of how you are going to get the parts done.

4. Work with other people – it can be more fun and make the work easier.

How long will it take?

Sometimes when we plan we make mistakes in guessing how long it will take to do something. If you have some homework to do as well as all the other things you want to do in an evening, you need to work out how long each thing is likely to take. This will help you plan to do everything that you need to.

7

Write down how long you think it will take to do the following things. Then time yourself, or get someone else to time you doing them.

	Guess	Actual time
Have a bath or shower		
Eat my tea		
Complete my homework		

How did you do? Were your guesses close to the actual time, or were they a bit out? If they were too short, you know that you need to allow yourself more time to get things done. If they were too long you know you can try to do more things than you are doing.

BUT be careful. Try to make sure that whatever you do, you do well.

Keep practising this – you will become good at knowing what you do and don't have time for.

7

Planning assignments

As you get older you will have larger pieces of work to do like assignments. I find a good way to start these assignments is by 'Brainstorming'.

Say the assignment is on the Ancient Greeks, here's what I would do.

1. Write the assignment title in the middle of the page
2. All around, anywhere you like, write down in pictures or words, thoughts and questions connected with the Ancient Greeks.

The idea is to sweep out your brain of anything you can think of to do with the assignment. That way you won't forget your good ideas because you will have a note of them and you can get them organized into some kind of order. You can do this by using a tape recorder. Try speaking your ideas and questions on to a tape. The main thing is that you have a record of them for later.

7

Ancient Greeks: Brainstorming sheet

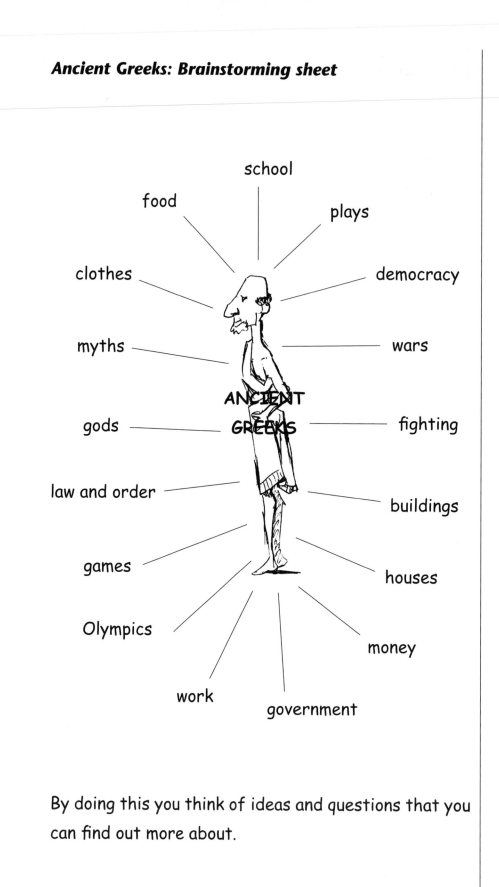

school

food

plays

clothes

democracy

myths

wars

ANCIENT GREEKS

gods

fighting

law and order

buildings

games

houses

Olympics

money

work

government

By doing this you think of ideas and questions that you can find out more about.

7

Brainstorming sheet

Use this sheet to brainstorm ideas for your own topic. Remember to write the topic title in the middle of the page.

7

Drawing up a plan of action

Now that you have done your first bit of thinking, and you have kept a note of your ideas, you need to plan when and how you are going to do the 'finding out'. This is where the work you did earlier, trying to guess the length of time it will take to do something, will come in really handy.

Here is an example of a plan of action:

	Lesson time	Lunch time	After school
Mon	Brainstorm. Decide on questions to be answered.		Surf the Net for info.
Tues		School library.	
Wed			Town library.
Thur	Discuss what you have found with your teacher and friends.	Decide which bits you want to use.	Discuss what you have found with your parents.
Fri	Get drawing, writing, tape recording, videoing and word processing. Remember you also have the weekend to work on your assignment. Completed and handed in on Monday.		

This assignment plan is for a short assignment lasting only one week. Now choose a topic and draw up your own plan of action.

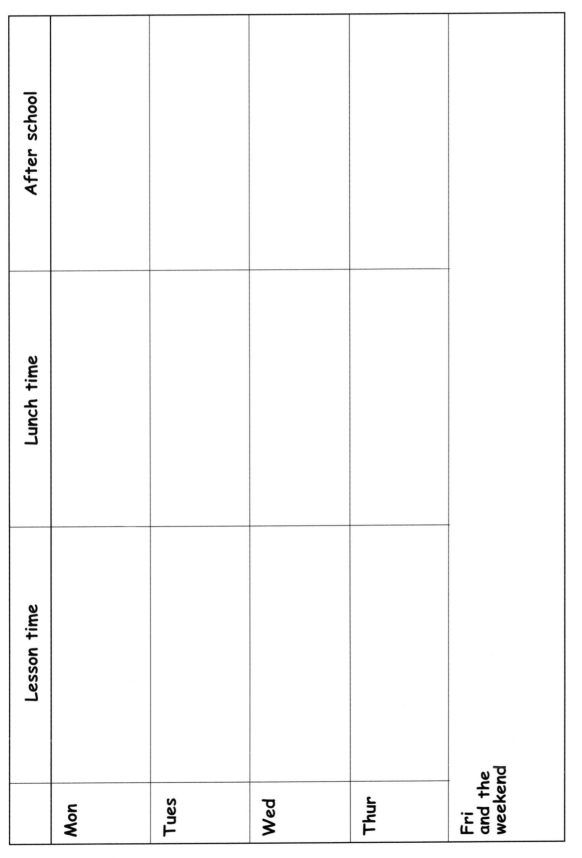

	Lesson time	Lunch time	After school
Mon			
Tues			
Wed			
Thur			
Fri and the weekend			

7

Once you understand how to draw up a plan of action for a short assignment you can try planning longer ones. When you do have a bigger assignment to do, you need to 'chunk' it. This means you split it into bits you can cope with.

Think of an assignment as your favourite treat. My favourite treat is a chocolate bar. Imagine the biggest size they do. If you tried to stick it all in your mouth in one go you wouldn't be able to chew it to eat it. So you need to bite off a chunk you can get in your mouth. If you do that it tastes really good. A big chocolate bar takes a few bites to eat comfortably. Sometimes you need a bit of a break in between chunks, you can feel a bit sick if you eat too much too quickly.

Eating a big chocolate bar is just like doing an assignment – take it in chunks and you will enjoy the experience, try to do it in one go and you could end up feeling sick.

Evening plan

Plans come in handy for other things too. To make sure you have time to fit everything into your hectic life make a plan for the evening.

3:30	Arrive home – healthy snack
4:00	Homework
4:30	Free time – TV, Playstation
5:15	Homework
5:45	Dinner
6:15	Jobs – washing up, tidy room
7:00	Practise music
7:20	Play with friends
8:30	Bath
9:00	Exercise – relaxation
9:20	Bed – reading and affirmation for the day

7

Now you try...

My plan for _____ (day of the week)

3:30	
4:00	
4:30	
5:00	
5:30	
6:00	
6:30	
7:00	
7:30	
8:00	
8:30	
9:00	
9:30	
10:00	

7

Is your plan the same for every day of the week, or do you need to make different plans for other days?

What learning and working style suits you?

Some people learn and work best listening to music. Some work best early in the morning, others late at night. If you know how you learn and work well you can use that knowledge to help you get your work done. You would be amazed at the difference it makes to work in conditions and at a time that suits your mind and body.

For each of the statements below choose a number from 1-4 and write it in the box.

1	**2**	**3**	**4**
Disagree			Agree

Say to yourself 'I learn and work best when...'

- ☐ I have just got up
- ☐ I've just had my lunch
- ☐ I've just had my tea
- ☐ Just before I go to bed
- ☐ I'm on my own
- ☐ I'm with friends
- ☐ I'm with an adult
- ☐ It's quiet
- ☐ There is relaxing music
- ☐ There is a lot of noise
- ☐ I'm lying down
- ☐ I'm sitting at my desk alone
- ☐ I'm sitting at a table with lots of other people
- ☐ I can get up and walk around when I want to
- ☐ I can write things down

7

- [ ] I can draw pictures as answers to questions
- [ ] I can read out loud
- [ ] I can hear instructions
- [ ] I can read instructions
- [ ] I can be shown instructions
- [ ] I have someone who can test me on my work
- [ ] I am sitting on a comfortable chair
- [ ] I am warm
- [ ] The light in the room is bright
- [ ] I don't want to go to the toilet
- [ ] I have had a recent snack
- [ ] I have had a recent drink of water
- [ ] I can get up and stretch
- [ ] I can make noises and talk to myself

The last two might sound a bit crazy, but if you watch people while they are thinking hard they do some funny things. The only snag is that while making noises might be great for the person making them they can be very distracting for everyone else in the room. Some things are best kept for homework!

You need to discuss these last two pages with your teacher and parent or carer so that they know how you work best and can help you.

Remember knowing when and how you work best is not an excuse not to work under any other conditions. It does mean you can help yourself, and others around you can help and encourage you to work when it suits you best.

GOOD LUCK!

7

A few final tips

- Start the day by standing in tadasana and say an affirmation to yourself.

- When doing something that requires a lot of sitting still and concentrating break it up with something to refresh your concentration. Try three calm breaths slowly in and out to help you refocus and get a little more oxygen to your brain. You may also find it useful to stand up and stretch tall, or you may need a complete change of activity, like doing a circle picture.

- Always remember you are better at a lot of things than many other people.

- Use your energy in a positive way.

- Learn how to relax and use the technique often.

- Remember some days will be better than others.

- Even when you don't feel great, there are still a lot of great things about you.

Congratulations

Congratulations, you have reached the last page!

I hope some of the things you have done on your journey through this book will have helped you to develop some good work routines so that life becomes easier for you, and so that people can see just how capable you are when you can keep your mind on things.

Remember if you know how your brain works, and by now you should have some idea about how you work best, you can work in ways that suit you. BUT you will have to make sure you discuss these things with your teachers and parents or carers, because they need to know how they can help you to do your best.

Good luck, and don't forget to let me know how you got on.

Email: katespohrer@hotmail.com

References

Anastopoulos, A., Barkley, R. and Shelton,T. (1998) The history and diagnosis of attention deficit/hyperactivity disorder. In P. Cooper and K. Ideus (eds) *Attention Deficit Hyperactivity Disorder*. Maidstone, The Association of Workers for Children with Emotional and Behavioural Difficulties (AWCEBD), pp. 21–29.

APA (1968) *Diagnostic and Statistical Manual* 2nd edition (DSM II). Washington DC, American Psychiatric Association.

APA (1980) *Diagnostic and Statistical Manual* 3rd edition (DSM III). Washington DC, American Psychiatric Association.

APA (1987) *Diagnostic and Statistical Manual* (DSM III, revised edition). Washington DC, American Psychiatric Association.

APA (1994) *Diagnostic and Statistical Manual* 4th edition (DSM IV). Washington DC, American Psychiatric Association.

Barkley, R. A. (1990) *Attention Deficit Hyperactivity Disorder: A Handbook for Diagnosis and Treatment*. New York, Guildford Press.

British Psychological Society (2000) *Attention Deficit Hyperactivity Disorder (ADHD): Guidelines and principles for successful multi-agency working.* London, BPS.

Cains, R. A. (2000) Children diagnosed ADHD: factors to guide intervention. *Educational Psychology in Practice* **16**(2): 164–80.

Cantwell, D. P. and Baker, L. (1991) Association between attention deficit hyperactivity disorder and learning disorders. *Journal of Learning Disabilities* **24**: 88–94.

Cooper, P. (1998a) Introduction: the reality and hyperreality of ADHD: and educational and cultural analysis. In P. Cooper and K. Ideus (eds) *Attention Deficit Hyperactivity Disorder*. Maidstone, AWCEBD: 6–20.

DFEE Publications (2001) *Promoting Children's Mental Health Within Early Years and School Settings*. DFEE 0121/2001. Nottingham dfee@prolog. uk.com

Epstein, M. A., Shaywitz, S.E., Shaywitz, B.A. and Woolston, J.L. (1991) The boundaries of attention deficit disorders. *Journal of Learning Disabilities* **24**: 72–7.

Hartmann, T. (1999) *Attention Deficit Disorder: A Different Perception*. Dublin, Newleaf.

Holowenko, H. (1999) *Attention Deficit Hyperactivity Disorder: A Multidisciplinary Approach*. London, Jessica Kingsley.

James, W. (1990) *Principles of Psychology*. London, Encyclopaedia Britannica.

Keller, W. D. (1992) Auditory processing disorder or attention deficit disorder. In J. Katz, N. Stecker and D. Henderson (eds) *Central Auditory Processing: A Transdisciplinary View*. Chicago, Mosby Yearbook.

Kewley, G. D. (1999) *Attention Deficit Hyperactivity Disorder: Recognition, Reality and Resolution*. Horsham, LAC Press.

Knivsberg, A., Reichelt, K. and Nodland, M. (1999) Comorbidity, or coexistence, between dyslexia and attention deficit hyperactivty disorder. *British Journal of Special Education* **26**(1): 42–7.

Maines, B. and Robinson, G. (1998) *All for Alex: A Circle of Friends*. Bristol, Lucky Duck.

Merrell, C. and Tymms, P. B. (2001) Inattention, hyperactivity and impulsiveness: their impact on academic achievement and progress. *British Journal of Educational Psychology* **71**: 43–56.

Merrell, C. and Tymms, P. B. (2002) Working with difficult children in Years 1 and 2: a guide for teachers. Curriculum, Evaluation and Management Centre, Economic and Social Research Council.

Munden, A. and Arcelus, J. (1999) *The ADHD Handbook*. London, Jessica Kingsley.

Norwich, B., Cooper, P. and Maras, P. (2002) Attentional and activity difficulties: findings from a national study. *Support for Learning, British Journal of Learning Support* **17**(4): 182–86.

Rafalovich, A. (2001) Psychodynamic and neurological perspectives on ADHD: exploring strategies for defining a phenomenon. *Journal for the Theory of Social Behaviour* **31**(4): 397–418.

Riccio, C. A. and Hynd, G.W. (1996) Relationship between ADHD and central auditory processing disorder: a review of literature. *School Psychology International* **17**: 235–52.

Richards, I. (1994) ADHD, ADD and dyslexia. *Therapeutic Care and Education* **3**(2): 145–58.

Richardson, A. J. (2001) Fatty Acids in Dyslexia, Dyspraxia, ADHD and the Autistic Spectrum. *The Nutrition Practitioner* 3(3): 18–24.

Stewart, M. and Phillips, K. (1992) *Yoga for Children*, London, Vermillion.

Still, G. F. (1902) Some abnormal psychical conditions in children. *The Lancet*: 1008–12.

Taylor, E. (1998) Hyperactivity as a special educational need. In P. Cooper and K. Ideus (eds) *Attention Deficit Hyperactivity Disorder*. Maidstone, AWCEBD.

Further reading

Developing Students' Multiple Intelligences (1998). Nicholson-Nelson, K. Scholastic: New York, USA.

Fatty Acids in Dyslexia, Dyspraxia, ADHD and the Autistic Spectrum (2001). Richardson, A. The Nutrition Practitioner (3.3) November, pp. 18–24.

First Steps to a Physical Basis of Concentration (1999). Anderson, R. Crown House Publishing: Carmarthen, UK.

Hyperactivity in the Classroom – A brief guide for teachers and parents (2001). Hyperactive Children's Support Group, HACSG, 71 Whyke Lane, Chichester, West Sussex PO19 2LD, UK.

Marching to a Different Tune – Diary about an ADHD Boy (1999). Fletcher, J. Jessica Kingsley Publishers: London.

Meditating with Children (1994). Rozman, D. Planetary Publications: Boulder Creek.

Parent Articles about ADHD (1999). Jones, C., Russel Searight, H. and Urban, M. Communication Skill Builders. The Psychological Corp: Texas.

Parenting the ADD Child (2000). Pentecost, D. Jessica Kingsley Publishers: London.

Promoting Children's Mental Health Within Early Years and School Settings. DfEE Publications. DFEE: Nottingham.

Ritalin Free Kids (1996). Reichenberg-Ullman, J. and Ullman, R. Prima Health: Rocklin CA.

Smart Moves (1995). Hannaford, C. Great Ocean Publishers: Virginia, USA.

The ADHD Handbook (1999). Munden, A. and Arcelus, J. Jessica Kingsley Publishers: London.

The ALPS Approach – Accelerated Learning in Primary Schools (1999). Smith, A., Call, N. Network Educational Press: Stafford, UK.

The Mindmap Book (1999). Buzan, T. BBC Books: London, UK.

Useful websites

www.borntoexplore.org

www.aacap.org/publications/factsfam

www.nimh.nih.gov/publicat/ADHD

www.healing-arts.org

www.youngminds.org.uk

www.hacsg.org.uk

www.adders.org

Supporting Children Series

These books are ideal for both teachers and learning assistants in specialist and non-specialist settings. Each book provides theory about a specific need, plus practical advice, support and activities to facilitate children's learning.

Orders

All these titles are available from your local bookshop, but in the event of any difficulty please order directly from us.

Orca Book Services
Stanley House
3 Fleets Lane
Poole, Dorset
BH15 3AJ, UK

Tel: +44 (0) 1202 665 432
Fax: +44 (0) 1202 666 219
E-mail: orders@orcabookservices.co.uk

For ordering information inside North America, please call 1-800-561-7704.

(PHOTOCOPY AND USE)

SUPPORTING CHILDREN WITH ADHD

2nd Edition

Kate E. Spohrer

A collection of practical suggestions and materials to use with pupils who have ADHD or demonstrate ADHD-type behaviour. This new edition is enhanced by two new chapters: one on the theory, medication and alternative therapies for ADHD, and one covering what the teacher can do, including case studies, an Individual Education Plan (IEP) writing guide and reflective questions for the teacher about the child and teaching strategies.

May 2006 * 112pp * Paperback * A4
0 8264 8077 2 * **£17.50**

(PHOTOCOPY AND USE)

SUPPORTING CHILDREN WITH DYSLEXIA

2nd Edition

Garry Squires and Sally McKeown

Supporting Children with Dyslexia focuses on the practical difficulties facing dyslexic pupils every day in the classroom.

This second edition now offers even more information, particularly on the definitions of dyslexia, perceptual issues, spelling patterns, remedial programmes, useful techniques, and dyscalculia.

May 2006 * 160pp * Paperback * A4
0 8264 8078 0 * **£17.50**

(PHOTOCOPY AND USE)

SUPPORTING CHILDREN WITH SPEECH AND LANGUAGE IMPAIRMENT AND ASSOCIATED DIFFICULTIES

2nd Edition

Jill McMinn

This book describes how these difficulties can adversely affect children's learning in both specialist and mainstream settings and suggests how the curriculum can be made more accessible to facilitate learning.

This new edition has been fully updated and now includes a photocopiable, task-based assessment chapter, and a suggested structure for Individual Education Plans (IEP) together with a template and bank of possible targets.

May 2006 * 192pp * Paperback * A4
0 8264 9103 0 * **£20.00**

continuum

Continuum International Publishing Group Ltd • London and New York • www.continuumbooks.com